THE AMAZON RAINFOREST

NORTHWATER

CONSTANTINE ISSIGHOS

Copyright 2012 © Constantine Issighos. Published in Canada. Printed in U.S.A. No part of this book may be reproduced or transmitted in any form or by any means, electronic or mechanical, including photocopying, recording, and/or by any information storage and retrieval system except by a reviewer who may quote brief passages in a review to be printed in a magazine, newspaper, or on the web without written permission in writing from the author/publisher. For information, please contact www.awaqkunabooks.com

NorthWater is an imprint of Awaqkuna Books Inc.

Vol. 6 of THE AMAZON EXPLORATION SERIES:
THE AMAZON RAINFOREST

Library and Archives Canada

ISBN 978-0-9878599-5-2

Library and Archives Canada Cataloguing in Publication

ATTENTION CHILDRENS ASSOCIATIONS, BOOK STORES, PUBLIC OR PRIVATE LIBRARIES: quantity discounts are available on bulk purchases of this book series.

THE AMAZON EXPLORATION SERIES

Children's Books
by
Constantine Issighos

1. Upper Amazon Voyage by River Boat
2. The People of the River
3. The Children of the River
4. Amazon's Nature of Things
5. Echoes of Nature: a Beautiful Wild Habitat
6. The Amazon Rainforest
7. Amazonian Sisterhood
8. Amazon River Wolves
9. Amazonian Landscapes and Sunsets
10. Amazonian Canopy: the Roof of the World's Rainforest
11. Amazonian Tribes: a World of Difference
12. Birds and Butterflies of the Amazon
13. The Great Wonders of the Amazon
14. The Jaguar People
15. The Fresh Water Giants
16. The Call of the Shaman
17. Indigenous Families: Life in Harmony with Nature
18. Amazon in Peril
19. Giant Tarantulas and Centipedes
20. The Amazon Ethno-Botanical Garden
21. The Real Amazon Tribal Warriors

In the Beginning…

There is an open boat moored by a riverbank in the Amazon rainforest. It carries a slab of mud taken out of the murky depths of an ancient lake. For thousands of years, this slab of mud was hidden deep within the maze of an Amazon watershed. Now it slowly makes its way to a safe place, holding twenty thousand years of biological evidence that research scientists will want to unravel. They all stand around it and stare at this lifeless blob of mud, wondering if, hidden deep within its bowels, there is a handful of pollen seeds, and a key to unlock the mystery that has haunted them for decades, the origins of the Amazon.

The term Amazon derives from the mythical Greek women warriors called *Amazonas*. According to the historian Diodorous of Sicily—second century B.C.—the Amazon region of the Greeks was an area of Northern Africa, including present-day Libya. This Amazon region was ruled by a gynaecocracy, which means that only women were qualified to hold high positions, including those in the warrior cast. The region was ruled by a Queen Myrina, whose army consisted of 30,000 female soldiers and 3,000 cavalry. They fought a number of male armies along the coast of North Africa all the way through to Egypt and Syria until, at the Aegean Sea, Queen Myrina fell in battle and her brave female warriors *Amazonas* scattered.

The mystery of the prehistoric Amazon of South America is one of the great unknowns. Contemporary research scientists know how the forests of North America and Europe were formed, and even much about the Ice Age that swept over Africa and Asia. But the Ice Age of the Amazon is still a mystery that needs to be explored. In this prehistoric past lies the origin of the marvelled biodiversity of the richest ecosystem on Earth. The current view of its origins is that the Amazon of the past is unchanged from its present. Species gathered in this southern warm and humid environment to avoid the dangers of the freezing Ice Age temperatures and to escape extinction. Only after it warmed did the plants and animals radiate back out again.

Geological History

Geological evidence shows that about 150 million years ago, the Amazon River flowed westwards—as part of the prehistoric Congolese river system from the interior of present day Africa. This was when the continents of most of the Southern hemisphere including South America and Africa, were joined as part of *Gondwana Pangaea.* When the Andean mountain range was formed by the collision of the two plates—the South America and the Nasca—this caused the formation of the Brazilian and Guyana bedrock shields. These shields, in turn, blocked the westward flow of the river, causing the Amazon to become a vast inland sea.

Gradually this inland sea became a freshwater lake, and the marine species adapted to life in freshwater. Due to geological changes, the Amazon Lake began to flow eastward rapidly draining to become a river—the Amazon River. About 100 million years ago, the ocean level receded enough to expose the land isthmus of Central America, thus allowing migration of animal species between the Americas.

The Amazon rainforest lies in the tropics between the Tropic of Capricorn and the Tropic of Cancer. In the world's tropical rainforests, sunlight strikes the earth at roughly a 90-degree angle resulting in intense solar energy. This intensity is due to the fixed length of the day at the equator: a steady 12 hours a day of the sun above the horizon throughout the year. It should be noted that geographical regions away from the equator have days of varying lengths depending on the season. In the Amazon region there are no distinctive seasons, just the rainy season and the less rainy season. This consistent daylight supplies the essential solar energy to power photosynthesis, which is vital to the plant life of the rainforests.

Since rainforests lie in the inter-tropical zones, where intense solar energy produces zones of rising air, they tend to lose their moisture through frequent and often strong rainstorms. Rainforest get at least 229 cm (90 inches) and in some areas over 10 meters (440 inches) of rain per year. In the Amazon rainforest there may be rain throughout the year without an apparent wet or dry season.

The Canopy Structure

The Amazon rainforest has a unique vegetative structure consisting of several vertically stacked layers including the *Overstory. the Canopy, the Understory, the Shrub Layer* and *the Ground Floor.*

The canopy is known as "the Roof of the World's Rainforest," and it refers to the dense umbrella of leaves and tree branches formed by closely spaced trees. The canopy is between 38 to 50 meters (100 to 130 feet) above ground level. Scattered within the canopy are even taller trees, 50 meters (130 feet) higher, which make up the overstory level. The understory is 3 to 10 meters (10 to 30 feet) above ground level. It is also known as the shrub layer, and consists of vines, shrubby and tree saplings. Ground vegetation consists of vines and saplings.

Additional plant types of the canopy system are the *Liliana* and the *Hemi-epiphyte* vines. The Liliana is a woody vine that begins its life on the forest floor and makes its way up to the canopy by holding onto the tall trees. The Hemi-epiphyte vine begins its life in the canopy and grows long roots that eventually reach the forest floor and can then access nutrients from there.

In the Amazon rainforest, the vast majority of the species have adapted to life in the leafy world of the canopy. It is estimated that in the rainforest 90% of the species that exist in the ecosystem reside in the canopy.

Complex Species Relationships

A key characteristic of the rainforest ecosystem is that all species are to some extent dependent upon one another. These interdependent relationships have been developing for millions of years and form the basis for the ecosystem. Therefore, when a species disappears from the ecosystem it weakens the survival chances of another. For example, the bee and its pollination of flowers- the bee needs and feeds on flower-nutrients and the flowers are dependent on the bee's pollination for their reproduction.

The loss of a keystone species—an organism that links many other species--may cause a significant disruption in the functioning of the entire food chain system. For example, the rubber tree seeds explode when they mature, thus sending them to the river where the vegetarian piranha and other fish crack the shells and devour the rich nutrients. Humans and other predators depend on these fish for their daily food intake. The elimination of the rubber trees may have a detrimental effect on the food chain of other species, including fish that feed on the seed-eating fish and the indigenous fishermen who depend on fishing for their daily subsistence.

The Amazon River

It is estimated that the Amazon River is the most voluminous river in the world. It contains eleven times the water volume of the Mississippi River and drains an area equivalent in size to the United States.

The river's outflow from *Cabo de Norte* to *Punto Patijoca* is about 250 miles wide, where its daily discharge reaches up to 505 billion cubic feet of water or 5,788.038 cubic feet/sec which flows into the Atlantic Ocean.

The Amazon's strong current carries 106 million cubic feet (or 2.3 million miles of land) of suspended sediment all the way from the Andes, some 4,000 miles, and discharges it into the ocean.

The waters of the Amazon River support a diverse range of wildlife, including the Pink Dolphin, Arapaima, the notorious Piranha, crabs, Giant Otters and Giant Turtles, the Black Caiman, Anacondas and the Electric Eel.

The Indigenous of the Amazon Rainforest

Contrary to popular belief, the Amazon rainforest has a long history of human settlement. Large, productive and complex societies existed in the Amazon rainforest. These societies maintained a natural balance between hunting and gathering clearing the rainforest for their family's agricultural plots, and managing the virgin forests to optimize the distribution of animals which were useful to them for food.

Of course, unlike current cultivation techniques, the original indigenous people were attuned to the ecological realities of their ecosystem. They had 5,000 years of experimentation to achieve a healthy balance, learning how to manage the rainforest to suit their needs.

Many of these indigenous populations lived along river and tributary systems where they had an excellent means of transportation, supreme fishing and fertile lands for agriculture. Unfortunately, when the Europeans arrived, these were the first settlements to be affected, since the Spanish and Portuguese also used the major rivers and tributaries on their way to the interior. Along with the explorers came the Jesuits and religious fanatics who, in the name of Catholism and with the blessings of the popes, began a long and tragic tradition of abuse against the indigenous people, one that would be continued by colonialists, rubber barons, loggers, gold seekers and land developers.

Amazon Historical Dates

1541—Francisco Orellana and crew explores the Amazon.

1637-1638—Pedro Teixeira takes the first voyage on the Amazon and reaches Quito.

1736—Charles Marie de la Condamine leads the first scientific exploration, opening the region to future explorers.

1800s—Alexander Von Humboldt explores the Amazon.

1800s—John Dunlop invents the tire, the rubber "rush" begins.

1800s—Amazon Basin becomes an important source of rubber.

1839—Charles Goodyear invents vulcanization.

1850s—Bicycles are very popular and increase demand for rubber tires.

1880-1895—Rubber barons get rich in Manaus, Brazil, and in Iquitos, Peru.

1890s—Exploration of the Amazon is conducted by the National Geographic Society.

1910—Rubber boom ends, cheaper labour and sources are found in Malaysia.

1914—Explored by Theodore Roosevelt.

1960—Brazil builds highways crossing the Amazon forest.

1982—Brazil sets aside 19 million acres for the *Yanomani* tribe.

1984—45,000 gold diggers pour onto Yanomani reserve lands.

1996—Main highway is constructed leading from Manaus to Venezuela.

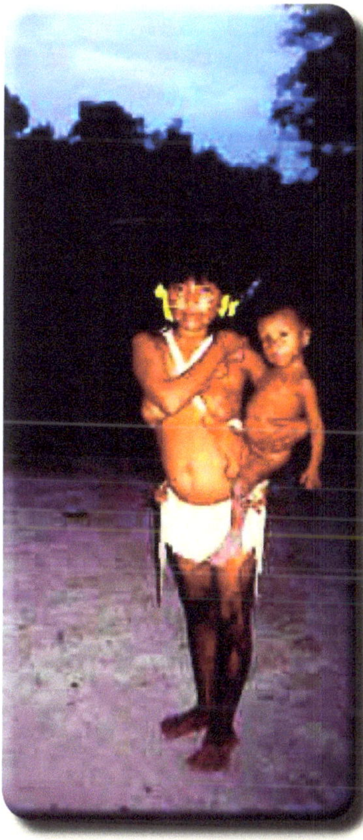

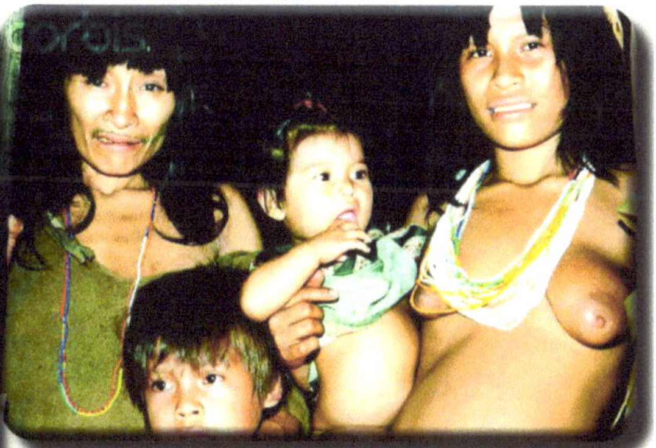

Not all Amazonian indigenous people dress in similar style. Families with children living close by a modern town tend to follow a western style dress code.

Indigenous families living in the interior of the Brazilian Amazon follow a more traditional dress style with prominent facial and body décor.

www.ingramcontent.com/pod-product-compliance
Lightning Source LLC
Chambersburg PA
CBHW041755040426
42446CB00001B/37